Singing for No Reason

by Andre Cruz

2019

Singing for No Reason

Copyright © 2019 by Andre Cruz

Cover Art: Kaique Rocha & Joanna Malinowksa

All rights reserved. This book or any portion thereof may not be reproduced or used in any manner whatsoever without the express written permission of the publisher except for the use of brief quotations in a book review or scholarly journal.

First Printing: 2019

ISBN: 978-1-7337455-5-0

i&R Publishing
7979 Broadway #209
San Antonio, TX 78209

https://iandrpublishing.wordpress.com

Ordering Information:
Special discounts are available on quantity purchases by corporations, associations, educators, and others. For details, contact the publisher at the above listed address.

To my mother Rebecca, and her mother Thelma, Adam, and Jenny Joy: Thank you all for loving me.

To Mickey Stocks, Jan Elliot, Terrie Tucker, and Shirley Cabada:
Thank you for putting the right books into my hands and becoming life-long friends.

To Jarvis:
Words can't describe how happy I am that you are here to share this moment in my life with me. I promise there are many more to come.
I love you.

To my dog Gizmo:
Thank you for being my companion, my rock, and sometimes the only voice of reason. I hope when all is said and done, I can give you 1% of what you've given me.

Lastly and most importantly, to those who are suffering through mental illness and/or addiction, those who are alone in this world and basically all the weirdos out there:
I wrote this for us and I have your back.

-Andre.

Singing for No Reason

1. Walking on the Other Side of the Road   1

2. We're off to see the Wizard…
But Not for the Reason You Think   11

3. I'm Freaking Tired of Waiting
for Paul Rudd   19

4. Are you there Nancy Reagan?
It's me, Andre.   29

5. Thanks for the Lovely Prayer…
Now Shut Up and Get into Bed!   37

6. When Did My Life Become
an Inspirational Quote?   47

7. Pipe Wrench   57

8. Intelligently Stupid   67

9. Life's Rock to the Forehead   79

10. The Woman Who Helped Me
Become a Man   91

11. Dear Future Husband
(Staple This to My Forehead)   99

12. The Darkness   109

1

Walking on the Other Side of the Road

I really can't stand those little tables they set up on the sidewalk in front of the gay bars testing for HIV.

I know, you're probably thinking to yourself, "Exactly what kind of virus spreading queen are you?"

Before you write me off though, hear me out. I can't stand them because I must avoid them.

I mean it's always the same routine: I see the perky little gay boy at the booth, with his arsenal of clipboards, pens, condoms, lube, and various other doodads to hand out for participating test takers.

I immediately think, "Fuck."

Simply because I've been positive for over thirteen years and don't want to bother with the fact that—still young as hell—I probably look like I should be approached about getting tested. They always let the older gentlemen pass by with a nod or a casual prompting about free testing. Suddenly, they see me or any other homosexual in the 18-34 age bracket (depending on the face cream they use) and they lunge into their assault.

Using myself as an example, they play the we're-instant-besties-so-you-should-listen-to-me tactic, which does not work on me at all. I'm an enigma, and a unique one at that; you can't just earn my friendship in five seconds. Yes. I know that I sound like a total bitch, and they are probably just concerned members of the community trying to do some good in a world of over-priced clothing and back-handed compliments; but the script is so tiring:

"Hiyeee! How's it going tonight?"

"Fine."

"Super! Would you like to take a free HIV test?"

"No thanks."

"Are you sure? Do you get tested regularly?"

"I know my status."

Singing For No Reason

It's at this point they go into final jeopardy and start the kind of instigation and guilt mongering that Catholic mothers can only achieve in their wildest dreams.

"How often do you get tested? Are you practicing safe sex? Do you have multiple sex partners? Are you attending sex parties? Do you go to the bathhouses? Do you engage in barebacking with a furry? Are you washing your foot before you shove it up a guy's ass?"

My initial response is to be a dick and say, "Fuck no, but damn how I wish!" However, being the Southern gentleman that I am I just say, "I have to go."

The absolute worst is when I am with other people, especially those who don't know my status, and I have to lie about recently getting tested at my own doctor. I mean I get my numbers checked on the regular so it's sort of true, right?

Let's face it, I'm not brave enough to be one of those guys that will hold up a billboard declaring his status for the world to see. Maybe someday, but just not now. So I lie. I get such an awful feeling inside. I just don't like to do it.

I know, I should just tell them I am positive, and they would back off. The few times I've tried this tactic one of two things have happened: they say things like, "Oh, I'm sorry," and without another word leave me standing there alone with my status; or they draw themselves up, give me a stern eye and say, "Please take some condoms."

They say it in such a matter-of-fact-you-are-part-of-the-problem-so-stop-having-sex sort of way that I'm left with a feeling of stigma that only another positive person reading this could understand.

Look, I'm all for promoting awareness; people should really get tested every three months if they are sexually active. Ideally, I would want everyone to have the initiative to take responsibility. It's such a sad commentary that we are reduced to these street-side Pinkerton's accosting people who are solely in search of a vodka and tonic. (Yes, I would like lime. Thanks!)

I'm just going to say so, right here and now! I do not want to have to explain to this total stranger that I was diagnosed three weeks after my twenty-first birthday. Nor do I want to admit that I never had the proper education about safe sex because one, I was gay and two, the sex ed. in South Texas was not as stellar as it is today. I feel like I fell into this limbo of time between the AIDS crisis in the 80's and the current recharging of the issue in present day. There was this relaxation of the issue with younger guys in my age group of gay kiddos. We never had to endure the horrors of losing someone we knew every week, just like I never had to come to terms with the fact that this insidious killer was coming for me and there wasn't a single thing I could do. I still sit in thought some days and wonder how something so tragic could be allowed to fade away. The fact that HIV was no longer a death sentence made a huge difference. Scores of guys were (and still are) thinking, "Well I can just take a pill if something happens," or, "I'm going to get it anyway so why not enjoy my youth?"

I was neither of these. I was ignorant, uninformed and just plain old not safe.

I was an idiot.

I remember being 18-years-old and spending Christmas Eve night at this boy's house. A boy whom I was desperately infatuated with but who only wanted some attention at the time. He lived with his gay uncle for a reason he did not divulge. Amid our naked cuddling, he casually mentioned, "My uncle is HIV-positive."

What in God's name prompted him to say so I had no idea, but I suddenly became very quiet. I remember feeling unusual; almost to the point of being repulsed that I was even in the same house as someone who was positive. Feeling a mixture of wanting to run as fast as I could and as far away from the stranger in the next room, but not wanting to leave this beautiful boy who was next to me…Like I said, I was an idiot. Three years later, I would be in this stranger's shoes…in his "house."

Before you post your opinion of me this very moment on social media, trust me; I got my taste of cosmic justice right after finding out my positive status.

After many nights of crying, drinking, and hopelessness, I decided this was my new lease on life. That this microscopic catalyst was going to help me take better care of myself. I feigned renewed strength! Revitalized! What a joke. Inside was a terrified little boy, not knowing where to turn next. Where the hell was Dixie Carter when I needed her?

I forged ahead with my gilded attitude and I soon met another boy. We did the usual tango of flirting and texting on our Nokia phones (boy, those were the days), and gave each other coy smiles. The thought of disclosure had crossed my mind a couple of times, but I was just too enthralled in the magic of pretending to be in a "normal" romance.

One night after a couple of weeks of quasi-dating, he surprised me by taking me to see a midnight screening of a movie that was only playing in my hometown, which was an hour and a half away from the big city. I don't really recall why, but that act of romance stirred something in me. A sudden feeling of dread and responsibility spoke clearly to me conveying one undeniable truth: I had to tell him tonight.

I remember we stopped at the local Wal-Mart to get a bulb for his license plate lamp. He was so astonished at my knowledge of changing such items on a car; (this kid had no real-world sense now that I recall). On the ride back, the silence I first encountered at that house made its comeback tour. Even to this day when I'm upset and deep in thought, I'm silent as a graveyard; a dead giveaway for my future boyfriend to begin his Barbara Walters interview about what's bothering me (cough, cough).

When we were three-quarters of the way back, I struck up an odd conversation. When I say odd, I mean way past left field, like the hot dog vendor's girlfriend's apartment behind the ballpark odd. I don't really recall exactly what I said, but I went the extremely long way around revealing my status to this kid; (I say "kid," but we were both the same age). I waited for his response for what seemed like an eternity.

He calmly pulled over to the side of the highway and I knew a shit storm was about to hit. He began yelling and screaming at the top of his lungs. I could only look down at the foot-well of the car after I had said my peace. I sat there and took the tidal wave of anger from this boy hoarsely yelling things like, "Murderer," and "Sicko." Mind you, we had only ever kissed and held hands; I was far too vulnerable to take the path of sexual righteousness with him. He kept going as if I wasn't there, as if no real person could be truly this angry in front of another. The words and emotions pouring from him were the ones reserved for the darkest places in our minds, never to see the light of day. Yet here I was, the proud new owner of them. He continued to shout threats of how I ruined his life, and how he was going to press charges against me. I held fast to my silence, with only a small stream of equally silent tears running down my face.

Finally, after he spent his rage, he demanded I get out of the car. I tried to be bold and stand up for myself but only managed to choke out a quiet plea to take me home. In a swift move that would make escape artists want to take note, he undid my seat belt, opened the car door, and shoved me out before I even could entertain the notion of fighting to stay. The last thing I saw were his taillights as he screeched back to civilization.

It was 3:00 a.m. and I was 15 miles outside of the city surrounded by a cloud of gravel and dust that was stinging my eyes now fully stocked with tears. God, it's a miracle I was ever romantic again. At that point, I thought of calling a friend to come and get me. I began to pull my phone out of my pocket, but how was I going to explain this? What had transpired. Why I was such a mess. I just slid the phone back down, thinking to myself how alone in the world I truly was, and that no one would show me sympathy to retrieve me from this situation. I had no choice but to put one foot in front of the other. It proved to be a slow and challenging process, but it was just me and the darkness. I looked up absentmindedly and observed a night sky that was full of stars competing with the lights of the city in the distance.

After about 10 steps I dropped to the ground and had one of the worst breakdowns of my life. (To this day it still ranks in the top 5.)

When the sobbing subsided, I picked myself up and started walking again. My mind began to wander as I tried to distract myself from having another breakdown. My thoughts went straight to him. The gay uncle, a man I never met but judged so harshly. That man who to this day and until that night, was a stranger.

He was now the man I had become.

Every day, during some part of the day I think of him and still feel extremely guilty for the way I felt that Christmas Eve night. Some nights, I lay there staring at the dark ceiling wishing I could find him. Wishing I could hug him and apologize for the evil thoughts he never heard. Wishing I could get on my hands and knees, crying for him to forgive me. I guess it's just one of those instances in life where you know you've fucked up royally and have no way of repairing it. This is a truth I must accept because now I know: The only place I'll ever see him again is the mirror.

2

We're off to see the Wizard...But Not for the Reason You Think

If you're positive, then you know lab (blood) work is a constant part of your life. To those of you who are negative, a normal positive guy in treatment will have his t-cells and viral load (among other things) checked about every three to six months. You would think after ten years that this would be a cinch, but no, I still dread it. Fear not, though! I'm not going to get into the gory details of why I dread it. (Sorry *Twilight* fans).

I will go as far as to say that it really isn't the needles that bother me, though they used to very much. Where those are concerned, I guess I just got used to the process. What I really dread are the feelings and emotions that go through me. You can pretend all you want that you don't have "it," and life is as normal as black and white TV, but when that needle is in your arm and the phlebotomist is filling vial after vial (my average is 8) you just can't pretend that much.

My ex used to get so mad at me, saying that I would ignore my "disease" as he liked to call it. I don't know, maybe there was some truth to those words. My philosophy has always been to keep it on the back burner and only take care of business when it was time to, meaning I'd go get my labs done and take my meds. Maybe because he never went with me to an appointment, he just assumed I was not handling my virus.

Come to think of it, I've never had a boyfriend or partner join me on this journey. I knew from the beginning that this was probably going to be a solo journey; there would be no Scarecrow or Tin Man to accompany me. As lonely as that sounds, I'm just not lucky enough for that and I must deal with it.

Overall, I think I've managed alright. I mean what other choice do we have? As long as there are Twizzlers and *The Golden Girls*, I can handle anything. I can tell you though, the first years were, to be frank, a bitch. The program I was in just ripped my innocent self to shreds.

Singing For No Reason

I remember being a scared little 21-year-old, sitting in that waiting room and anxiously listening for my name when it was my turn to see the doctor.

Like it was yesterday, I remember talking to myself and saying things like, "You're okay now, the doctor will know how to save your life," or "He's going to help you get through this."

Well the person I got dealt was a nurse practitioner, a female, a lesbian. Now this is my disclaimer: the fact that this person was a woman and lesbian is not a generalization of any woman or lesbian (Insert the "Some of my best friends are women and lesbians" argument). But how can I describe this woman? You know one of those people who just hates every one that is the opposite of them? In this case the objects of her despise were men, and in my case gay men.

Not to get my foot too far deep into my throat, I'll simply let you know that every time I saw her over that first year, I became more and more depressed.

The nurse would always spout these off-hand comments that made me feel idiotic for catching this super easily avoidable virus, evil for insisting on finding love after the fact, and lesser than her because I had to depend on her. As I write this and think back, I'm still trying to come up with excuses for how she treated me the way she did. The most I can come up with was that it was her version of "tough love." However, I keep bumping up to the fact that I was neither an alcoholic or drug addict (at the time) that needed some kind of reinforcing catalyst to change my life for the better; I had just been a scared little boy who gave my heart to one who would do him harm.

Sure, it sounds like I am still holding a grudge, but I learned a long time ago just to let things like that go (an ongoing lesson to this day…). I eventually left that clinic, and on the recommendation of an acquaintance, went to another hospital system. There I found a caring staff and an amazing doctor. One who healed more than just my body, but also my faith. I have since moved to another city and, after some more trial and error, have found a medical team close to what I had in those early years.

The other day, I went in for my labs and sat in the waiting room listening to Wendy Williams in the background. I looked up from my Huffington Post and saw two young men, who I assume were boyfriends. They had to be about 22. Without staring too much, I gathered one of them was there to "take care of business." The other was supporting him with smiles and humorous chatter. I silently hoped inside of myself that one of these boys could

Singing For No Reason

be spared. Sadly, I also must admit that I did feel a little bit of envy, for I never had that kind of support. Luckily, before I got too reflective and began looking like a total psycho, the nurse called my name. I left the pair the way I approached them, as a nameless stranger.

I walked a little slower down the hall to the lab, just thinking… I was able to shake the feelings off and walk into the lab of phlebotomists.

Let me tell you, I don't know what it is, but these people are the best. Always cutting up in one fashion or another. Maybe it's just me but every lab tech I've met is a real character. This certain instance was no exception: I walked into the scene already in production, where the heroine was scolding a boy in a joking manner. As I sat down to wait my turn, she led her mystery companion out of the cubicle.

It was a boy about the same age as the couple I had seen earlier. This poor guy had fainted when she attempted to take his blood. Of course, the lab tech was just teasing him, while simultaneously confirming he was okay. She made sure he replied to her in a conscious voice, retrieved him juice, and made him laugh.

Turning to me, she asked my name and said, "Okay baby it's your turn, and don't be pulling the same shenanigans. I can only handle one at a time."

She smiled as she spoke and upon examination of the young man, I saw what was so funny. The kid was like 6'4". You can see the comedy in that, can't you? A big, tall, strong young man like that fainting was like the Cowardly Lion all over again.

I replied, "You don't have to worry about me; I'm a pro at this, and I've got over 10 years to prove it."

She repeated, "10 years" back to me, paused for a moment and then continued to tease-check on the young man. All the while smiling. However, I suddenly noticed a certain sadness in her eyes. I found that so curious, until it hit me.

It was his first time.

I am so thankful she stuck my arm at that moment because I probably would've broken down crying if she hadn't. I gave her a weak and awkward smile, and she just went about her business. Sassing me like no other. I realized the sadness wasn't just for him, but for me as well.

She finished, and I thanked her. I got up with my little Band-Aid on my arm and walked to the door. I was only able to nod to the young man, though my heart wanted to give those boys so much more.

Everything in me wants to sit down with them all and tell my story, tell them the trials I've survived, and the hope that was available to them. That if someone like myself could survive, they could surely do the same.

When I was a kid, that acne medication Proactive infomercial would come on late at night. I remember the first spokesperson, Judith Light (who played Ryan White's mother, Jeanne White, in the made-for-TV-movie, "The Ryan White Story." There's your history lesson for today kids). Light gave her closing statement about having suffered all her life with acne and how she would see people, mostly young people, all over the place with acne. She expressed that she always wanted to say something to help them but stopped herself because she didn't want to embarrass them. Lastly, she commented about her regrets for doing nothing.

Now I know exactly how she felt.

When I got into my car, I just put both hands on the steering wheel, closed my eyes and leaned forward. That's all. I just sat there in silence for a good ten minutes. I am quite proud of myself for not crying.

You know, during those first few years I would sit in those waiting rooms and see gentlemen older than me. No matter how hard I tried I couldn't help but look them over. Some were perfectly healthy, others not so much. I would think to myself, "Will that be me someday?"

It was this day in the car that I realized I don't resemble the young men anymore. I couldn't help but wonder if they had noticed me, if they saw me as some older crystal ball. If they had the same thought I did: "Will that be me someday?" I'll never know, but maybe someday when they are my age and see a kid in their situations they'll be braver. When it's their turn.

For what else can we do in life…but wait our turn.

3

I'm Freaking Tired of Waiting for Paul Rudd

Of all the "four-letter words," love is by far the worst, and it's probably why you hear about it more than the rest. From the day we are born until the day we die, love seems like your only true goal. Love is such a non-word though; much like the word "normal," it has no set definitions, and sadly, for some of us, there are no definitions at all.

Yep, you guessed it, I've never known love (insert the "nah you have to had known it at one point or another" argument).

Don't get me wrong, it's not that I grew up not wanting love. Most of my adult life has been spent looking for it under every rock, tree, and gay bar. Understand I speak of the romantic kind of love. I know that I am loved and I love others, but when it comes to the love of a partner or soul mate…I…I just don't know.

As any "normal" gay boy I had my share of celebrity crushes from TV and film. They would come and go as was my fashion. However, the one and only devotion of my heart belongs to Paul Rudd. As the waves of embarrassment come crashing down, I will opt out of going into much detail except for saying that his method of acting always struck me as something tangibly relatable, for lack of a better term. In my mid-thirties I just wonder if that kind of man is out here in the real world.

When I think of the characteristics I ask for in a mate, I tend to gravitate to ones that are internal. While I can appreciate, "tall, dark, and handsome," I'd exchange that for, "humor, kindness and understanding," any day.

Thus, I began my search. Which proved to be…I'll get back to you when I find the appropriate term. Though not entirely a negative experience each time, my relationships would always come to an unavoidable end. The problem was that I would always convince myself that what I had in any relationship was love, when it really wasn't. What

Singing For No Reason

was surprising was that I was avoiding love, but more on that later.

Despite what your friend's Facebook page tells you, finding true romance is hard. Not to mention when you throw HIV into the mix. No matter how you acquire your life-long viral companion: through betrayal, unintentionally, or any other means, love just takes a back seat I guess. Your panic and self-doubt control the show. Not to mention the now difficult subjects of disclosing of one's status, deciding on whether you want to date only positive or only negative people, and so on (I could go on all night). The quest for love is suddenly turned upside down. Yet, despite it all, we keep trying for love, repeatedly. We search endlessly for that one person to make us feel "normal" again, to make us forget what we now are, to heal us. Now, I myself can only speak as a gay man, but like they say, "love is love."

I will tell you two stories.

For myself, I used to dream as a young boy of who my husband would be. I would have dreams at night of us camping in the woods, having coffee and breakfast, and taking trips together. Keep in mind I was about seven years old when this would occur. Growing up in the country I had my share of trysts with straight boys who were merely experimenting. To be honest, it was hell. Being so alone, I was off to a bad start in the rat race of love.

Fast forward to my young adulthood, there was one failed relationship after another. My friend Cooper used to kid me that I was always looking for that picket white fence. Towards the end of my 20s, I started finishing his statement with "so I could burn it down." I was that discouraged. However, it was curious that most of the fault for the failed relationships was my own. You see, I had spent a lifetime hiding the fact that I suffered from depression and anxiety. I also actively denied my true self because of a ridiculous fear of rejection. I became extremely good at wearing a mask to the world. That mask sadly came with a price. If the only person that people who were attracted to me got to know was a mask, then they never knew the real me. When you don't know someone, you don't trust them. Where there is no trust, there is no love. I became borderline delusional, starting to believe the mask was my identity.

Now you mix that mask with HIV and you have a very defeated young man. I started to believe that love just wasn't for me. I gave up. Let me tell you folks (are you listening over there in the back?), the day you give up on love is when the world turns into a dark and scary place. I decided I was only good for the physical, and random hookups were my religion. Not a healthy lifestyle indeed.

Then came the last man to date the mask.

Singing For No Reason

Albert was a gay man, but he grew up in a time when every man was expected to marry a woman and produce a family. He had a small taste of love in the beginning but was betrayed and scared into conformity. He soon married a woman, one to whom he confessed his true self. That truth was used against him, and over twenty years he was abused repeatedly both verbally and physically. Yes, and even sexually. Albert's wife would blackmail and threaten to out him whenever she wanted another child. She had one of those baby addictions (think Octo-mom), and they ended up with 6 kids. In my opinion, that is rape. Plain and simple. As you might guess, his life was filled with much despair. He tried his best to cope. He dove into his work and became obsessed with material possessions. Anything to fill the humongous void in his life. I still wonder to this day, how you could be surrounded by so many people that were supposed to be family and still be so alone. It breaks my heart to the point of tears every time I think of that fact. So Albert and his wife eventually came to an agreement: She would go and do her own thing, and he would go do his.

That arrangement though, just wasn't enough for him, and he gave up. Even though we have that sad fact in common, we both gave up at different times. You see, I gave up after I was diagnosed. Albert gave up and sought out the virus, a snail-like suicide if you will. Life, as it does in the current moment, showed no signs of changing for either of us. That is, until an unusually warm day in January.

Some random guy I had hooked up with before wanted to meet up and asked if he could bring a third. I said sure, I mean what the hell did I care? The random guy got there, and I said I was going to shower while he waited for his companion. All clean and ready to regret my choices, I emerged from the bathroom and came to a full stop. Unsure of what to do I stood there for an eternity holding my breath. Time resumed, and he asked to use the bathroom. All the while I was thinking he was going to find an excuse to leave after seeing me. Little did I know he was thinking I was going to ask him to leave after seeing him. Not to get too into the nitty gritty we eventually lost the other joker and spent a great non-sexual time together. He said he needed to get home, and I mentioned I'd like to see him again. Surprisingly, he replied the same but looked as though he didn't believe me.

Then came our first official date, seated at a restaurant outside, and, surrounded by people, I told him my story which I thought would surely run him off. Then something happened. That man, that beautiful soul named Albert told me his story with tears in his eyes. He sat across the table and woefully told me how this would never work and how everyone before me had usually gotten up and left.

He then became much more emotional and said I was now allowed to do the same. I got up. He began to sob harder, but I didn't leave. I moved to the chair next to him and took his hands, stating I wasn't going anywhere. You see I had never witnessed such beauty in my life, such bravery. Thus began our journey.

Can't I tell you the truth (since you know, it's just you and I…)? We ruined it completely. I had idiotically given him the mask to love, even though he saw past it. The first person to ever truly see who I was underneath, and I gave him the same stupid dog and pony show. The difficulties were not all mine though; he walked away from the only life he had known for over twenty years, and there were many instances he would run right back (miserable as it was). I constantly paid for crimes that the one before me had committed and added to my sentence crimes I committed myself. We both wanted to be happy for once but made it much harder for each other.

Although a little embarrassed, I must admit we are now just friends. Still, the fact of the matter is that when I finally embraced myself, I was able to make someone happy if even for a short while.

I am grateful for my time with Albert because now I define love as a big fucking responsibility and something I no longer take lightly. My experience with him made me realize how utterly exhausted I was carrying that mask for so long, and that all I had to do was let go. Now that I was truly alone, I was finally able to tear down the wall. All the bricks I had spent more than a decade laying, one after another dissolved instantly, allowing me to rebuild and reinforce myself the right way for once. That's what they don't tell you: how much work true love takes, not because you are now responsible for the love of another person. No, it's much more than that.

You see, that's the problem. We search, and we search for that one special person and never realize there are actually two. We go out to every bar, we use Grindr like a divining rod, or we join churches and choirs for all the wrong reasons. We spend so much time focused on finding that one individual that we forget to find someone more important to love. Ourselves.

To love ourselves and others we must really know ourselves and that is where the work of love truly begins. Knowing, trusting and eventually loving ourselves and never allowing that love to yield by any means. Now, it may be easier for people living without HIV or it may not. Who am I to say? What I do know is that when I finally got to know myself, love myself, loving someone else started to seem like it will be that much easier. So, to the HIV positive young person that is about to give up: I hold out my

Singing For No Reason

hand to take hold of yours and tell you that I love you with all my heart. I love you, and need you to find yourself, to love yourself, so that you can love back. I mean, Paul Rudd is going to need it when my true love eventually takes his place.

4

Are you there Nancy Reagan? It's me, Andre.

Did I ever tell you about the time I got addicted to Crystal Meth for nine months? No, seriously. It's such a tangled web of a story I don't even know if I want to write this chapter. That's how we deal though, right? Where to begin…

I guess we should go all the way back to when I was 23. As you previously read, I was desperately trying to find love and looking, not only in the wrong places, but in dangerous ones. My first boyfriend had lost his job and met a young man who partook in Crystal Meth. One day I came home and the new one was sitting on the couch with a duffel bag. I was informed that he was moving in and I had a month to get out. Anyone with half a brain would've walked out, but I was so desperate and praying for a miracle that I stayed the month in a one-bedroom apartment. Meanwhile, they stayed on the couch having sex and smoking Meth while I was in the other room. I know.

After that experience, I became somewhat of a snob towards anyone who did any kind of drug. I did not associate, date, or even sleep with anyone who did drugs (Yes, even Marijuana). I avoided them all like the plague. Now suddenly, I'm on the other side of the table and I promise you I feel like the world's biggest hypocrite. Not to mention the universe's biggest asshole.

So, let's time travel back to present day. As recently as last year, I was in a toxic relationship. Only after I had relinquished my own apartment and moved in with him did I discover his severe alcoholism (He drank 1.75 liters of vodka a day!) and also his history of problems with Crystal Meth. Don't take this as blame towards him, at least not totally. I mean I saw what was happening. The days were getting longer; his abuse towards me got worse and worse, and the will to live was vanishing. He indirectly introduced the wonderful solution of Crystal Meth, and I reached a point where I no longer cared about anything or anyone. Most importantly myself. I threw away all the love that was available to me.

Forgive me for being so graphic, but you need to understand the gravity of the situation. I began by smoking Meth, as most people do, and within a couple of months, I was injecting myself. To give you a picture of how much I didn't care about myself, I have always been deathly afraid of needles, like "Richard Pryor" afraid (Google it, Millennials). Yet, here I was shooting up Crystal Meth daily for close to six months.

I'd like to say that I overcame this problem on my own and was able to live another day to fight the good fight, but no, I would probably (and I'm not being dramatic) be dead right now had it not been for a handful of best friends. All the love and strength they give/gave me, without asking a thing in return. I mean, don't for one second think that this is a tale with a magical story-book ending. Far from it. For you see I'm writing this only being sober for a month, but you need to know. I need to tell you.

I've hurt people, mentally, emotionally, and yes, even physically. So much so, that people don't recognize me anymore. The truth is neither do I, and that terrifies me. This whole situation has created a monster inside of me. Another identity. I sit here and wonder how the hell this apparition, this phantom Andre could exist. Was he always there? A dormant side of me that used this drug to gain his emancipation? What scares me the most is when I lay awake at night and wonder, is he here to stay? There ~~were~~ are times when he takes the controls and the good man that I thought I was gets locked inside, forced to watch through the windows of my eyes. Screaming, begging, pleading tearfully for the phantom Andre to stop. For you see, that one never regrets what he does, he doesn't care who he hurts, and he never has to pay for what he's done.

I do.

Don't despair, I mean things are better, but I feel they will never be the way they were before one stupid "yes" ruined my life. Perhaps that's what I need to accept, because the person I was becoming before Crystal Meth had led me to say yes in the first place. Maybe if I make it out alive through this ordeal, it will make me stronger, and make me love fiercer. I'll let you know.

Let me take this moment to say that even though I was self-medicating and not stealing to fund my habit or craving the drug every five seconds, I am an addict. The second you start diminishing the problem is the second you convince yourself that you don't have a problem, and then guess what?

Singing For No Reason

The thing that really sucks about this whole mess is that I've come out (so to speak) to my friends and family about being an addict, and once you step through that door everything changes.

Everything.

People who are ignorant about addiction don't know how to act around you. Kid gloves, eggshells and awkward turtles are all bulk ordered through Costco. You disappear for more than five minutes and people automatically assume you're doing drugs. People say they care, but they have no idea where to begin, so they just give you space. Lots and lots of space. So much so that you can easily misinterpret it as abandonment. Suddenly, you're incapable of taking care of yourself, anyone else, or even your dog. Why does this suck you didn't ask? Because I deserve it. I deserve every single fucking bit of it. Something I have to live with.

I'm not going to endorse or condone any single method of recovery. One process is not the solution, for we are all different. I'm doing alright though: I'm seeing a psychiatrist, and soon a therapist. I take my medication, am going to group meetings, and I've decided to go totally sober.

Totally sober? You may be sitting there and thinking to yourself, "It must be hard to give up things like alcohol too. Why so extreme?" I will tell you why: Because the beast has been awakened and is now looking for any portal through which he can take the controls. No cocktail is worth having to watch and see the total terror in your friend's eyes. That image is so burned into my memory that I get physically ill if I focus on it too much. Trust me, that's enough to keep me on the right track for a lifetime. I don't think I'll ever forgive myself though, because my friends tried to empower me, and I just threw it away at the time. The friends who are still around believe in me so much that I can't bear the thought of losing the only loved ones I've ever known. I can't bear to have them believe they were wrong because right now, they see something I only used to see, someone I want to see again.

The sad reality is that mine is not a unique story, but people just don't know how common it is. It's like a whisper campaign taking the good people of the gay community one by one (insert paranoid conspiracy theory comment, cue Julia Roberts). A former acquaintance put it best when he said Crystal Meth is going to be the AIDS epidemic all over again. And I believe him 100% percent. I mean, Nancy Reagan saw it coming, and people laughed at her. Hell, they still do (try Google again). Now look at us…

People always ask me how it was that I could have so much access to the drug if I was

Singing For No Reason 35

unemployed (another wonderful side effect of the drug). The answer is simple for two reasons. First, in my part of the gay world you can practically trip over it. It is so accessible. Too fucking accessible. Secondly, this is a lonely drug. You have all these users floating around who have lost everything, so they are more than willing to lure people in similar straits by sharing their drugs. They end up building faux friendships that dissolve once the well runs dry, or if someone hits rock bottom and/or meets hard times. Trust me, I've seen it with my own eyes.

The other problem is, once I tried to rejoin society, I received ridicule from so many people I had called friends and acquaintances. People were shocked at how much weight I lost and judged me disgustingly about using drugs without letting me get a word out of my mouth. I'm not mad by any means. But that's because I used to be one of them and I pray none of them have to learn the hard way like I did. So, what the hell can we all do? We are all children, and we need saving.

You'll notice that I haven't used any slang when referencing the drug, and that's simply because we need to call Crystal Meth by its name; we need to stop hiding the horror of this drug with cute names or references. I'm also not going to tell you not to do drugs, it's not my job. That would be like being in an old 50's horror film and telling you not to go into "that" house. Of course, you're going to wonder what it's like to go in. I will tell you to appreciate what you have. All the friendships, love, life, income, good coffee, drag queens, food, and shelter. Everything. One yes could wipe it all away faster than you think, leaving you alone. Alone with only an altered, disgusting version of yourself to keep you company long after you finally get some sense to stop (if you're that lucky). Go out and reinforce what empowers you.

Ironically, my first boyfriend always used to say that in this world we are either assets or liabilities. Please take it from a liability: Stay an asset.

5

Thanks for the Lovely Prayer…Now Shut Up and Get into Bed!

Religion and I have been in a "junior high," romance all of my life. Going back and forth year after year. Sometimes forgetting each other or faking interest at other times. Well actually, I was the only one doing the forgetting. This is a very heated topic and I'll understand if you want to skip ahead, I mean the old me would. You'll miss out on the free nachos though… just saying.

My family was never very religious growing up. We were what you called "Easter-Christmas" Catholics, if even that. You see, religion and the

Hispanic patriarchy are very intermingled in South Texas. My mother had always gone against the grain of the patriarchy, (getting an education and a career) and later, when my parents got divorced, against the grain of the church. You can probably guess that our church going days went from scarce to nil.

However, the church still influenced my life in other ways. You see, my mom's house is across the street from the Catholic church we affiliated with the most. I must confess I used to love going to bingo as a child. The paper calling cards, the liquid stampers, the lucky charms and amulets. That's where I coined my not-so-famous phrase, "I was jumping up and down like an old lady at Catholic bingo."

One day the priest was transferred out for embezzling church funds and taking trips to Vegas or something like that (I really don't recall most of the story I must admit because I was a child). He was soon replaced by a Polish priest who was a very strict and cold man. He brought a discipline never seen at our small-town Catholic church. Among other radical acts he instantly shut the weekly bingo games (I know right?!) stating that they were solicitation. Curiously to me though, the ads in the weekly program increased from one small page on the back to several pages and squeezed into any space available.

Now this didn't bother me directly, but it was at this very moment in my life when I began to question religion, and for that matter question God. Why was one solicitation permitted and another not? Ugh! I was such a philosophical nerd. As the years passed by, I began to spend less and less time at the House of God across the street. They even had security tell us to leave the church playground, which my siblings and I had played on most of our lives.

Soon I sought out other places of worship, not as places of worship but as places to pass the time. I was acquaintances with some of the Methodist and Baptist kids in school choir, so I would join them on summer programs or vacation bible schools. No surprise to anyone I stuck out like a sore thumb. I'm not sure if it was because I was Hispanic and most of them were Anglo, if I was not religiously "right" with the Lord, or if I was the gayest thing this side of the Rio Grande.

There was something about these kids that was so peculiar to me; they came from mostly happy families (on the outside at least), they didn't fight, they were clean and pressed. Most of all they all were happy, and that happiness seemed to come from belonging to something bigger than themselves. Even with all of these differences, they were friendly to me. I never really felt excluded. That is, until the parents got involved. The parents always seem to deter me from speaking my mind or getting too close to their church. To this day, I have never figured out why. Eventually their children grew into adults who followed suit.

I moved on and out of my hometown, heading to the big city. Who needed God? As I look back, I now see how serious that statement was. The seriousness was then compounded by my HIV diagnosis. Where was he? Why didn't he love me? Why did he let this happen? You know, the usual blame shifting. I continued my journey without him, not that I let him join me all the way earlier on.

Year after year went on, and I became more depressed and anxiety ridden. As I reached my 30s, I moved to an even bigger city and sang in a men's choir as I had in the previous city. This choir though, was affiliated with a gay friendly church. We sang at several services and some of our own members' funerals. I watched the members of the church each time. I noticed the same characteristics as I did with the religious kids. I was, however, an "adult" with my own "I know I'm right" opinions of things (most of which were dead wrong). I scoffed at the members, thinking to myself honestly that they were fools. Clinging to an upbringing and a God who rejected them. Mere conditioning, I told myself. I went about my business convincing myself I was smarter than religion. Smarter than God.

Singing For No Reason

Big. Mistake.

My life was so empty. A void. No love, no purpose, no life at all. Well, where there is a void, you search for things to fill them. Most times in the wrong places and with the wrong things.

Enter Crystal Meth.

You've read it. I wrote it. Let's shove in the "needle" in deeper though, shall we? Oh, there is so much to tell, but I've got to stay focused. I got so deep into the drug because I had no one to guide me. No one to take my hand and lead me away. No one to love me even then, and when I say love, I mean beyond the physical and emotional. No, I needed a love so much deeper. I was so fucking stubborn. I still didn't listen. Even after I made friends, I flagrantly bragged to them about being an Atheist. Of course, they didn't believe me for a second.

About half way through those eight months, something happened. Something I regret ignoring. There was a run-down corner store in the neighborhood I was living in. They didn't exactly cater to the best clientele, but what did I care? I was now one of them. One day, I went in for some sports drink or something (I can't really remember). I looked a wreck (I hadn't showered in days), I was high, I was a mess. This old man, I'd guess he was in his seventies, was in the store. I know this is going to sound totally odd, but it felt like he was waiting for me. The reason I say this is because he noticed me the second I walked into the store. He approached me without fear and said, "Con Dios, te puedes salvarse de la Crystal.

"With God, you can save yourself from Crystal Meth."

Weird right? It was to me at the time, but not so much anymore. I gave him a "get away from me weirdo" look and left the store quickly. He watched me as I went.

Months passed, I decided to attend the Easter service at the gay friendly church with Albert. It was not my idea of a good time, but it was his first holiday without his family, so I wanted him to be in a safe space. I had been mostly sober for about two months. I know this sounds totally cliché, but the sermon sounded like it was written for me. That is, my ears perked up. And though I shrugged it off at the time, a small part of the message was left with me.

More time passed, and I relapsed, eventually having an overdose. Albert took me to the ER and then kicked me out. I had nowhere to go. I was about to drive myself to get high somewhere, but thankfully I stopped myself and drove to where my choir rehearsed. Not knowing what to do, they called around and on the suggestion of someone I did not know, they sent me to a psychiatric emergency room.

I have to say—even with my flair for drama—this was the absolute scariest twenty hours of my life.

You see, the room was almost completely dark (think like a photographer's darkroom), comprised of two rows of ten recliner-like chairs. Chairs [deep breath] that were filled with every level of psychiatric patient imaginable. From people screaming to people crying for no reason, to people running around naked saying they were going to kill everyone. They also had a movie playing in the front of the room. An extremely loud action movie—which was not the most calming in my opinion. That was my prize. A prize for living the life I had, I won a seat in that room. The psychiatric nurses were like you pictured them: brute gentleman that were overworked and undercaring. Still coming down from the Meth, I instantly freaked out. So much so that I was deemed a danger to myself. I got an even more special seat close to the nurse's station with the other poor souls. I wasn't allowed to use the bathroom with the door closed; I wasn't even allowed anything but some hospital socks and a thin blanket. They eventually gave me medication which turned me into an unfeeling zombie. Curiously it was almost the opposite feeling of being on Crystal Meth. I was slowed down to 1 mph and was forced to watch through the windows of my eyes. Unable to do anything about it.

I got seated next to a very angry man and a Hispanic guy who was covered in tattoos. The angry man started focusing his anger on me, stating how dare they seat a gay guy next to him, that I probably had AIDS, and that if I came near him, he would kill me. The Hispanic guy came to my rescue though, telling Mr. Anger to leave me be if he knew what was good for him. Surprisingly Angry Guy stopped. The Hispanic guy quietly told me his little brother was gay and to just ignore him and get some rest.

So, I did.

What I mean to say is that's all I really could do. I put the blanket over my head and tried to sleep. As long as I laid there, I still couldn't sleep. During that period, I was examined by two psychiatrists, who didn't really seem concerned with my welfare at all. Just another Meth head they had to deal with to earn their living. After the second one saw me, I was ushered back to my chair and returned to my blanket fort. I began to sob silently.

I was alone.

No friends, no boyfriend, nothing.

Then the most surprising thing happened: I heard a voice. At first, I thought I that I was going insane (thankfully I was in the right place for that [insert sarcasm]). The voice told me to calm down and I did. The voice was neither male nor female. It was more encompassing that anything. It told me I was going to be alright, that I would make it out of there and out of addiction. That all I needed to do was follow them. It was at this moment I stop breathing and went cold.

God was talking to me.

Upon reflection, I now know that God had sent many "representatives" (for lack of a better term) to try and get my attention but like I said I'm stubborn. So much so, that he had to make the visit himself. And on the day God pays you a visit, you offer him coffee. I kick myself so much that all I had to do was shut up and listen. I could've spared myself a lot of hurt and hurt to others if I had just loved myself, loved Him.

I made it out of the ER and back into life, I got help and began attending the gay friendly church every other week. Still, after all of this, the sermons seemed catered to me and me alone. As I stated before, I always felt like my life had been missing something. Maybe this was it.

The final call came on Juneteenth. God sent one of his most important (and I must say most beautiful) servants to give a guest sermon. As she spoke, I felt so humble…released. So…free. The words she gave and energy she brought as she spoke them struck something in me. Something that had been dormant all my life. Something that belonged to God. The voice of sarcasm that God had given me now thought to himself, "Okay, now he's just showing off." God wasn't showing off though, He was just showing me how I had made the right decision. I finally was loved down to the cellular level where his creation of me began.

I'm still not the most religious of people. I don't know if I'll ever be. But I do know that he and I are on this journey together. I know I'll never be alone again.

There is a Jason Robert Brown song entitled, "Music of Heaven," a song which explains my situation perfectly. There's a line that says, "When will it open my heart/when will I open my heart." The answer is simple: when you let it. My grandmother used to say when referencing God, "It's only a test." I always wondered what the true answer was to this test.

I finally figured it out: the answer is…to let go. Let go right now and just love.

6

When Did My Life Become an Inspirational Quote?

Regrets are tricky to process in general. I mean yes, sure there are the easy regrets.

"I regret having that chocolate cake."

"I regret not learning French."

"I regret the last thing I said to someone."

But in my case, and I'm sure pretty much everyone else's in the room (Well…except for that one dick in the corner that has it all together. Yes, I'm talking to you, sir.), regrets become a tangled headphone cord that's been in your pocket all day. It's not that my regrets are that much deeper or more important. No, it's more along the lines of the meaning behind those life-changing regrets.

For example, when I say I regret not practicing safer sex in my youth; what I'm really saying is, that I regret not respecting myself or my body enough and paying the ultimate price in the end. When I say I regret my past relationships, what I'm really saying is, that I regret not loving myself first and putting in all the work that it takes to make the relationship a success. When I say I regret becoming addicted to Crystal Meth, what I am really saying is that I regret…I regret giving up on every aspect of my life and becoming totally responsible for becoming a monster and a risk to myself and the people around me.

I could go on all day (you know me), but what I'm getting at is that I think most of the time we don't take the time and effort to dig deep enough to find **why** we regret the things we do. It's like when I'm an uncontrollable sobbing mess, instead of telling myself to just stop crying, I really should be asking myself, "Why are you crying?" (Though hell, sometimes you just need a good fifteen-minute sob in the park. You just do.)

Insert that pathetic cliché about hindsight and such, but how do we prevent regrets from happening? There's no manual, and every life journey is completely different. There is no way to see every sight at every Disney Park in one trip folks, no matter how well you plan. My grandmother always used to say, "If you want God to laugh, tell him your plans." You know, how you don't really get the deeper meaning of love songs until you've had your heart ripped out and [insert blunt instrument of destruction]. Regrets follow the same pattern, you don't regret something until that moment you realize your life is lacking just that very experience. They can really build up if you let them too. That's dangerous baggage to carry around when you're interacting with the world. Regrets are the gateways to severe depression, anxiety, drugs/alcohol, and—at their worst—suicide.

Right now, you're thinking, "Gosh do you only always dwell on the negative?" In a quick reply, I say unto thee…quite the contrary. You see, it is my firm belief that everyone must resolve their regrets in their own way. We simply cannot pass around a cheat sheet for the exam of life (more people fail at it than you think).

Luckily, most times there are make-up exams if you have figured out your individual way to deal with not only the regrets, but the reasoning behind them; you can make peace with or even reverse the regrets by doing/saying/experiencing/loving/living what is and was meant to make you a complete version of yourself. Yes, I know you cynics in the audience (I'm club Vice President, we're looking for a Treasurer) are saying it's a pipe dream to want to be able to have as few regrets as possible. However, through a lot of self-reflection and action, the path to whiter whites can be achieved.

Look, this isn't my guide to living life to the fullest. Please! I barely live life to the 1/16 on any given day. I haven't found my secret ingredient so-to-speak, but I know that throughout the experiences I've gone through and the meditation on them; I will make that 1/8 mark before you know it. Hell maybe 1/4 by the time I'm middle aged. You know my motto: Shins are the limit.

I know I'm being a little facetious, but I'm trying to show the obstacles I've had to overcome, and one of the major ones has been my inability to think and believe I deserve that 3/4 (see, I'm still doing it). It's not as simple as just saying, "I'm going to wake up tomorrow and believe that I deserve that much of life." Some parts of a belief system almost seem like genetics when you're caught in them. Much like you can't change your eyes from a beautiful steel green to an understated mahogany, believing differently can be a monumental and taxing challenge. I always find it funny, nay annoying as hell when those people who already believe the way you want to, advise you to just believe it. Just like that. Well it's not so easy. I mean we never get

Singing For No Reason

upset about cutting people off on the interstate until we're the ones getting cut off. You must let people make changes in themselves in their own way. My little gay sappy ass must learn how to slay the runway in a 3-inch high heel in a 13w. To say here you can do it in a 9 is just as awkward and painful as someone saying just, "do it," a certain way.

Don't misinterpret, you should always support those you care about. Go ahead and counsel and advise all your little accomplished heart desires. But in the end, you must realize that people will have to make their own decisions and do it in their own way. So, what's the point you ask (Oh, wait. You didn't ask? You're looking for the restroom? There's one on each end of the store, whichever one you choose to use is up to you.)? The point is by offering your experiences and wisdom (whether by learning from your mistakes or successes) you help that person realize the true secret weapon to battling the life-long nemesis of regret.

What is that secret weapon? Dare I tell you? It's a simple answer. Something hidden in plain sight, the back-door handshake. An "If you have to ask…" sort of thing. Okay, fine. I'll tell you, but simply so you'll stop blackmailing me with that video of me at eight years old playing wrestling with my siblings and cousins swinging around that Loaded Purse. Jesus, it's a wonder I didn't become an interior decorator, choreographer, or event planner…dare to dream I guess—

The secret is: time.

Yes! My friends, that's all there is to it. When you get to this epiphany that you have time to correct the regret—a fact that's as old as the hills (or as old and worn out as most of our excuses for our regrets)—you can begin your Modest Mouse, 'Float On,' adventure to regretless living. Time is where you can also get to the root of what caused your regret in the first place. Time. Good ol' double-edged sword time. Yep, you can abuse time if you get too comfortable in the knowledge that time will always be there (you know like squandering love and understanding by subconsciously taking advantage of the fact that you have so much love and understanding). And abused time is one vengeful bitch. Once you run out of time by wasting it, you get that super heavy flow of regret. You ain't wearing no two-piece bathing suit with it. Yet again, you must learn that simple common-sense fact on your own. (I'm a smart guy, but I am the Flava-Flav of common sense.)

Tell ya what I'll do, I'll throw in a bonus ingredient for overcoming regrets if you sign up for the email list (Oh no, we don't send out *a lot* of it [malevolent laughter]). The bonus ingredient is (cymbal crash): accepting responsibility. You simply

Singing For No Reason 53

cannot blame your regrets on circumstances or on other people. The only person regretting your regrets is you, cupcake. (Okay, well maybe your mom too. Though you really should have become a famous successful doctor/singer/actor/inventor, I mean she did warn you.)

In all seriousness though, I must own up to the fact that I am responsible for contracting HIV, for not appreciating and nurturing true love when I had it, and for destroying my life with Crystal Meth. Accepting responsibility for my part in my regret is another major part of getting past it.

If you hold your ear to the shell, you'll hear a lot of denial and projection with people. Folks can't 'fess up, stand up and say "Yes, I was a fucking idiot and I alone did the damage." They just won't do it, no way, no how. Some will even go as far as focusing so much on making *others* own up to *their* mistakes, just so no one really puts the spotlight on themselves. You know who you are, but you'll never admit to it. (I kid.) (Well not really but I'll never admit to that.) Now, taking your half of the check called Responsibility is a thankless job. In my experience, no one ever really cuts you any slack when you stop, take a deep breath and say, "That was my fuck up and my fuck up alone and I'm dying inside." I guess just a fact of life, meaning I don't want to get too much into it without pissing off too many people (Ma'am put down that pitch fork!).

One last thing, you need to realize that some regrets are irreversible, and the actual events surrounding the regrets you'll have the next morning will have happened so fast and snowballed so quickly that there was really no way to avoid them. You hurt yourself, you hurt others, and there isn't a damn thing you can do about it. You can only work forward learning from your not-so-shining-what-the-hell-possessed-my-unstable-total-risk-of-an-ass-to-do-that mountain of a mistake. Once you accept the fact that there was nothing to control the situation, and harmoniously own up the fact that it was all you; the sooner you can hold up that rear-view mirror dangling from one cord, get it fixed, and get back to moving down the highway of life, you know the one without the functioning HOV lane.

Again, like I said earlier, this is not the new trend in dealing with your regrets. It's just based on my experiences, which are no greater or lesser than any of your experiences. I am far from joining the regretless elite, I still have a lot of work to do, working late nights and holidays even. With regrets and their untangling, I try to apply my life philosophy of do unto others, but I do it one better by adding more: Give compassion to someone else's regrets, with special regard to ones that you know nothing about. Be understanding, not only of where the person's regrets led them, but more importantly how those regrets came about. It's totally your choice though. Just don't want you to regret not doing so. Especially if you end up in a "Who Wore Regret Best" situation, where you said you would never be caught dead wearing that outfit…

So, when you see those people trying to pull off a certain look, just remember: That could be you. Then again, maybe it already *was* you and nobody ever told you. If you don't believe me, I have the video file to prove it.

7

Pipe Wrench

You cannot tell a dog, "Be less of a dog!"

Yes, even if he's whizzing on everything possible in the apartment. You can only ask him to be a dog outside, which is still kind of offensive in my opinion.

"No Fido, you can't do that here, go twirl outside where it won't stain."

Yes, I know as millennial-sapiens we can't have our Pomeranian-Pug mix (is a Pugeranian a thing?) eliminating indoors. Can you blame them though? They are just being themselves.

I find that this theory relates to my life now and the life-long journey of finding my true self. Heck, you can pretty much apply it to any surface and watch how the boat doesn't leak. Order now people!

You see, early on my unique expression of the human spirit was very apparent.

I was born in the middle of a parade, true story. My mother always tells me of the day I was born and how her mother looked at me, then turned to my mother and said, "He's going to be different."

Gramo replied, after Mom asked her what she meant, "He's just going to be different, and you need to make sure he knows that's okay, and you love him the same."

And that children, is the day my grandmother laid her curse upon me…just kidding Gramo. No really, it was a joke! Please put down the yardstick…ouch! (Got to love those John Paul II era Catholics.)

Back to the topic at hand, by the time I was a preschooler I would sing Expose's "I'll Never Get Over You Getting Over Me," at the top of my lungs. I put on original plays for my mom and sisters (playing both male and female roles in full costume), and I walked with my hands up and on my toes.

Singing For No Reason

Of course, my mother was supportive through it all, loving and beautiful like she always was, always is. However, my father (the biological one) was a different story. A textbook example of the Hispanic machismo, he believes that men rule the world as men, and women are inferior creatures. Women's only purposes: the reproduction of heirs and production of hangover food (because staying out at the bar until 3am is a perfectly acceptable thing). Then came me. Oh honey, you have never seen someone pretend they didn't have a son like this before! Too make a long reproduction story short, he has about 56 (8) kids from his first marriage, and three from my mom's temporary insanity of marrying him (Yes, I'm going in deep. No prisoners.). He has three boys, born in a row. I'm the middle son…oh, the irony.

So, my little fabulous ass was slowly coming into my Wonder-Woman-like powers as a young child, and he just couldn't deal. My mom once asked him to let me have piano lessons and he said no; stating that it would make me gay. Well I guess I showed him!

He flat-out refused to have a son like me, and he took on the monumental task of correcting the issue. To him, the compressor just needed to be changed out and the coils needed a good flush (He's an HVAC tech by the way.). We then began what I like to call, "Cody's Reparative Therapy and Air Conditioning Repair." It began with my gestures. I was too flamboyant for my own good, so he made me walk around the backyard for hours in a circle, carrying a pipe wrench in each hand. I'm not talking about a crescent wrench or pair of pliers you queen! I mean the Super-Mario-Bros.-Wile-E.-Coyote-Roadrunner-Acme cast iron kind of wrench.

There I was walking in circles repeatedly (a tiny foreshadowing of self-fulfilling prophecy. When I say, "Story of my life," people, I mean it!). What was curious was at first, I was excited to perform this task. I mean who wouldn't want to be trained to be a big strong man at the age of six? The reality, however, soon set in as my hands, arms, and heart all began to hurt. It's amazing how I can vividly remember dropping to my knees one day. No tantrum, no big production, just tears in silence. I think this was the day I made the connection between what I was being made to do and how it was used to deter, to suppress, to eradicate my true self. In this one moment, that six-year-old boy discovered he had no place in this world. Every day I wake up and for the briefest of moments I still feel the way I did that day, like a little boy lost. So utterly lost in a world that would not have him.

The statement is totally absurd, I get that now. Right about now, you are saying to yourself, "Why didn't you say anything?"

I know I should have refused. I should have thrown that wrench back in his face, rather than throwing it into the plans of my life. I should have told him to fuck off when he suggested I wear my left and right shoes on opposite feet to see if it would correct the way I walk. I should have gotten in his face, foaming at the mouth, and told him I was who I was born to be and he either could accept it or pack his shit and go; but come on...

...I was six.

And he was my dad. My appointed role model and hero. I trusted him, and he dropped the ball. I think by far that is the deepest disappointment I've ever experienced (yes, even more so than John Travolta in *Hairspray*). I got a head start on the hard lessons of life, and things haven't changed at all with him; he's still the same. My parents divorced when I was twelve, and he's had several girlfriends since, one failed relationship after another. He's a really smart guy, so much potential left neglected (guess his training program was a success after all). I call to say hello or wish him well on the holidays or his birthday and get the same script:

Cody: Hello?

Me: Hey Dad, how's it going? Happy Birthday!

Cody: Thanks, I'm okay. Who's this?

No, I'm not fucking kidding. Every time since I turned eighteen he asks who is calling, three sons and he asks. I was home visiting last week, having breakfast at my favorite taco shop/gas station. He walked in, walked past me and sat down in the booth behind me (mind you, he hadn't physically seen me in three months) [deep breath]. I don't want to get to a point where this turns into a chapter about him. It's not. It's about me. Me, me, me, me, me. I'm just merely trying to display the impact his actions early on (and later in life) had on the man I became, or should I say *didn't* become.

Since that time, I have actively rejected the true person inside. Leaving only a shell to be filled with one meaningless faux self-image after another. Repeatedly, walking in circles. Even regarding relationships, I would just bend my will to that of my boyfriend's. Very *Runaway Bride*, "How do you like your eggs prepared?"

Like being on a carousel (I don't like merry-go-rounds, too much variety to choose from...go ahead and roll your eyes), riding round and round with your true self standing stationary at the outer gate. Each time you pass him he's waving trying to get your attention, then he's jumping up and down, next he's got a flight traffic controller's baton in each hand (where he got them from beats the hell out of me), but with each lap you ignore him. Suddenly you are about to make the turn again and you think to yourself, "Hey, was that me?" Now you eagerly wait to verify your true self is there to meet you.

But he's gone.

You spent so much time trying to find the right horse to ride, you ignored your true self and he exhausted what little energy he had left. He tried and tried to get your attention but ultimately gave up, walking away in resignation. Guess what! Ride's over. Now what are you going to do?

Yep, that's how I got to where I am today, the secret to my success. Seriously it's so upsetting that I want to throw the laptop out the window. I'm a thirty-four-year-old man who has no clue who he is or what defines him.

Thankfully, I've realized this fact before it's too late. Don't misunderstand, I'm still going to have my *Citizen Kane* moment whispering, "Celine…" on my deathbed. Just for kicks.

Holy crap is it hard learning the controls again! Thankfully the glitter drive was in mint condition. It's been a slow process, and one with repercussions. Today many "familiar" people just don't know who

I am, and now that I've once again started coming into my own, some of them just are not down. I'll admit that stings, but it's like I say with my recovery, "I ain't got the time."

Baby either you ride with me to Andre Town or you stay put, but the train is leaving the station with or without you.

Please forgive me if I get a little upset when people ask for me to tone it down, pull it back, or change who I am completely. I've just spent far too much of my life holding it in—the biggest insult to my Creator I might add. I finally figured out that he knew exactly what he was doing. She knew that the world was going to turn into a tumultuous and dangerous place. Where unspeakable tragedy would become the norm on the nightly news and the utter obliteration of the Earth was slowly becoming a feasible reality, in God's infinite wisdom, the universe knew what had to be done: I needed to become who I was really made to be...

For I am a secret weapon and an answer to the world we live in today. It comes down the truth of one of Allah's many purposes for me while on this planet:

Laughter.

I am here for the comic relief, the ray of light in the storm.

I'm meant to be too much, say too much, and go to the ends of the Earth to make someone smile. My plumes are extravagant to remind you that there is still color. I am being directed, nay compelled to throw on a wig and Mexican house dress, get in a river and make a video to make the world laugh. Yes! Everything must be comical in my life! There is humor in it all. It's what keeps me going, but I can't do this on my own. To make people laugh, I need people to stay around and laugh. Supported not thwarted. So please, I'm begging you, don't disappear when I give my best ballet performance in the middle of Target, don't walk up behind me and put unbelievable force down on my shoulders trying to get me to walk flat footed. Don't tell me to tone it down, rolling your eyes and saying, "Oh, Andre." Please don't, because even though you mean well, all you're really doing is handing me another wrench to carry. But if more of us could only be who we were made to be, making each other laugh and bringing out the child in that sulking, stern person over there, just imagine how much the hardware sales would drop! I've decided to do my part.

I know you get this, it's not that hard. Hell, on some level even my father gets it too.

When I was 18, I was brutalized by my little brother and sent to the emergency room. My mom drove me, but upon hearing the news, my father rushed right over. He asked my mom to step out and she did. He looked down at a bruised and extremely bloody man. He stroked my hair and began crying (the only time I've ever seen him cry). I looked him in the eye through my sorrowful and blood shot eyes. He reached over and held my hand, and before they could even administer pain killers I closed my eyes and gently fell asleep. There was no hospital, there were no injuries or tears. Just a dad holding his six-year-old little boy, whom he loved more than anything.

I guess people's thoughts about us are more complicated than
they look.

8

Intelligently Stupid

"Hey, do you want to come over and have a game night?"

No. No, I do not. Absolutely and definitively, I do not want to take part in another game night, and one other thing…we do not validate parking! Good day, Sir (Insert otter meme)!

I'll tell you why, I'm just too smart for my own good. I can't help feeling a little narcissistic in making that statement, but there is no other way to describe my intellect. You see, when I was a child and in my grandmother's care, I was very much alone. My grandmother decided to take me to the library and make me read 5 books a week. I immediately dove into the inexhaustible world of books and they soon became my reason for being. So much so that I had a 9th grade reading level by the 2nd grade.

You can say it: "What's your point, nerd?"

My point is that throughout my life I've been at a different level of intellect than my peers. What's worse is that I fail to comprehend how things that are easy for me to understand are difficult for others. I mean, seriously. Anyone who's anyone knows what a compound modifier is, right? Hello? Anyone? No? [sigh] Okay.

More on that later, but let's get back to "Game Night" shall we? My main problem remains that games are all about three things: comprehension, application, and competition. Spending the first thirty-three years of my life alone and devoid of real human interaction, allowed me to hone in on these skills in seclusion. Much like a Buddhist Monk detaching themselves to achieve Spiritual Enlightenment, I became very good at games, puzzles and video games. As I write this, I can remember being seven, and playing myself at Candyland; I can also remember being 25 and playing Clue with my Yorkie. (I let him win though, he's a bit sensitive.)

Singing For No Reason

Let's just face facts: People do not like others who are smarter than they are. Once they realize you are different, that you find no enjoyment from pointless Facebook videos, that you have a musical appreciation that goes beyond today's top 40 or actively avoid the latest Melissa McCarthy film in which she plays the same idiot, they go into their Pod Person, "Not One of Us" ritual. In truth, they begin to resent you.

The same goes for game night, once you prove yourself easily victorious, no one wants you to play again. For myself, this became such a regular occurrence that I began adjusting my playing to lose on purpose in the hopes that people would like me. But that didn't exactly work out the way I had envisioned. You see the conundrum was that it took the fun out of the game for me. On the other hand, if I played to the best of my abilities, my opponents were robbed of their frivolity. Besides, the result left me with was such a bitter taste because they only enjoyed an altered and false version of myself. By now you know how much I can chew a problem until the flavor is not only gone, but the original ingredients have disintegrated. So you can image how much thought I've given this. At this point I've only been able to come to one conclusion: Some people do not like me when I'm myself.

Not to say I'm a bad person. I mean there are no body parts in my freezer (touch my lime sherbet though, and you will end up taking its place in pieces), but there is something about the very core of me that turns some people off. I can't help but sit and wonder why. Am I just being overly sensitive? Am I borderline Asperger's? Is it all in my head? (at this point I say to you, "Not one word"). The real problem though was my realization that other's aversion applied not to only the gaming world, but to all aspects of my life. Especially in love and friendships, I have continuously dumbed myself down to fit in. I haven't utilized my word bank, I've forcibly laughed at those videos, I've discussed celebrity gossip as if it were a critical current world event, and I've hated myself through every second of it. I just haven't been authentic, and it hurts.

Now you want to pat me on the shoulder and give me a "There, there..." pep talk. You want to fill to the limit with cliché advice "To thine own self be true..." Blah blah blah. Or you want get up and leave, as so many people like me have been left behind when things got too hot. You're gonna give me "tough love." You're gonna get someone else to do that "listening" job since spitting out shoulds and should'ves was your only ace. But save it. When someone feels like they have no alternatives at all, your shiny pedestal won't do them any good. Here, it's either join the unwashed masses and blend in the way everyone wants or stay alone. I think, "All I can be is alone, just me and my brain." (But you can see he's kind of a dick though—to me and to everyone else.) And no one knows what how to help. No one can comprehend.

Deep breath. I'm sorry, I know I sound like a total self-serving asshole right now, but I'm just so tired. I am drained and exhausted from trying to find a solution to this problem: I'm open to suggestions. What's worse is that I find explaining this to others falls on deaf ears.

I play a lot of Words with Friends and I win every single game. It's boring. A very "One Man Punch" situation (Google it Gen X-ers). I was complaining to Alan that I was tired of winning every game, and how just once I'd like to be beaten by somebody in a true challenge. He replied sarcastically, "Go ahead Andre, please continue telling us how smart you are…" I then went to Facebook and made a post about how I hated being so smart, to which I received a reply about kissing my own ass. Sigh. (The big reward for building yourself up when nobody else will…)

But please tell me why it is socially acceptable for someone to say, "I'm tired of losing every game and just once I'd like to beat someone in a true challenge." Is broadcasting your losses really the foolproof way to make and keep friends? What if you really need someone to support your wins? Anyway trust me, being intellect-smart does not automatically make you a winner, at least not in the aftermath of the game. Win too much and it makes you is lonely, undefinably lonely.

The hardest places for me have been relationships. Things will be going well (well enough at least) and I begin to trust the person with my dark nerdy secret. I trust them, and start to ease my intellect in, but it always backfires. Sadly, this has happened so many times that it's practically textbook by now. The other person changes in a way so odd that I can't explain the metamorphosis. Perhaps it just reflects their insecurities with their own intellect. Maybe they see the real me and decide I am not for them. Who's to say? All I know is it hurts, more than anyone could imagine. The absolute worst is when they begin to use my intellect as a weapon against me. During disagreements or an argument, I get phrases like, "Well I don't know what to tell you, I'm not *smart* as you," and "Whatever, I know you're lying, you're smart enough to make up something like that," or "Yes Andre! We all know you're smarter than everyone."

"Tell me something Brainiac, if you're so smart, then how is it you could be dumb enough to contract HIV or get hooked on Crystal Meth?" Now that's a question.

Singing For No Reason

denied her intellect. Guess the suppressive apple doesn't fall far…

As the class went on, I would correct the professor several times remotely (he was video conferencing from another city), and my mother would get after me for doing it. She informed me that I was being totally disrespectful, but knowing how crucial a passing grade was to my classmates, I just couldn't sit idly and let him miseducate them. I was also suspicious that he would remain blameless while at the same time marking them incorrect should they answer the way that he taught them. The professor got a little flippant with me, telling me more than once that I was mistaken, and HE was correct. Yet he would always come back to the next class apologizing and saying that I was indeed correct. It wasn't because I was right that I thought this was amazing, though; it was because he was actually willing to admit his error. Still I noticed how increasingly scared my classmates were getting after each class. One woman was even on the verge of tears and feared losing the teaching job she'd held for 25 years. Something had to be done!

So I did what any sweet smart guy would do: I set up two tutoring sessions before the mid-term and final. I got permission to use the classroom on a Saturday and I stood in front of the class and began to help them in any way I can. Both sessions were hours long and tedious work, but the efforts were so rewarding! Every single person passed the class, and my mother at the age of (the following age has been redacted to preserve my lifespan) walked out of that class with a 90. To this day I've never been prouder of anyone. What was even more rewarding was that they all valued and appreciated my intellect. I was finally celebrated for who I was in my entirety. So I'll bet that's the key. I can't just *own* my talents, I need to *use* them in the things that matter to the people that matter to me.

So the theory says at least. I just wish I knew how to apply my passion and capability in that tutoring situation to everything else that defines me…

So how do I get back on the road? Will I ever make it to the Promised Land of Andre? Will people ever accept my intellect fully? (Will *I*?) Are there enough snake bite kits in the reflection/therapy ambulance of this life? All this and more to come right after these messages…

9

Life's Rock to the Forehead

[Big breath] Okay on this day in history…I'm not going to be dramatic. As most of my stories start out, there I was minding my own business. The evening was a dark and stormy shade sprinkled with the flicker of lightning and a symphony of thunder. Okay, not really. It was actually a sunny day, and I was in the fourth grade. While on our lunch recess I was (it shouldn't surprise you) completely alone. This was the usual routine for me throughout grade school. Suddenly, I felt a conk to the forehead and heard a metallic knock to accompany the thump. It didn't exactly hurt as far as I could tell, though. The bell rang and I began my lonely trudge back to class. A kid pointed out that there was blood gushing from of my forehead. A teacher soon appeared and ushered me to the school nurse. I don't remember much, just that it turns out a boy had thrown a rock randomly and struck me by mistake. They ushered him in and made him apologize. The boy was sobbing (and to be honest I think they had just yelled at him, which was a little extreme in my 10-year-old expert opinion), and he said he hadn't meant to hit me. I replied saying that he didn't do anything wrong and that I wasn't mad.

Whenever I reflect on the event, I always rub up against the same "what if" scenario: What if I had been playing with friends on the playground instead of being off by myself? Perhaps I would have never been hit by that rock, or become HIV positive, or gotten hooked on Crystal Meth. But speculation is just that, speculation. For I've never had my own group of close friends (plot twist, yeah?). Friendship has always been mysteriously elusive to me and I'm not sure why. I mean I did just what the purple dinosaur told me to do (and trust me, he has what's coming to him)!

The only platonic relationships I've had have mostly been acquaintances. That's as close as I've gotten. I would've been okay with this, but that damn Bette Midler was so insistent. Oh yeah and I did have an imaginary friend named Quigley, but he eventually took a job in Fiji (He still writes every now and then).

That's not a sob story, I swear (pay no attention to the fingers crossed behind my back). I'm just trying to say I never figured out the secret of friendship and have never experienced the full benefits. To make things worse, I've foolishly tried to make friends by offering too much. Lending kids my car in high school, giving money freely and basically going beyond extremes to get people to like me. It's a shame so many have taken advantage of it.

When I was a young adult, I was at a party in another city. I met a handsome guy about my age. We talked, and though it was no romance in the making, we agreed to stay in touch. For the first year or so we spoke almost every day on a primitive instant messenger. That was a particularly lonely time in my life; high school was over and there were no extra-curricular activities to distract from my having no friends. Believe it or not, this guy got me through it. In my eyes, he made me feel that someone cared, if only electronically.

Fast forward to present day, where I ran into the guy about 10 years later. He was in extremely bad shape, actively using Crystal Meth and homeless. Now here is the part where I tell you that my maternal grandmother and mother have always taught me to give back love and kindness, no matter what anyone did to me. That said, I had this complete urge to help him and pay back what he had given me. I gave him money, I fed him, I let him stay in my home and gave him one of my used iPhones. I eventually discovered that he had feigned friendship just to survive. He took my money without thanks, he slept with my roommate (ex-bf) and even tried to convince my roommate to kick me out so they could be together. He also sold the phone for more Crystal Meth. But the ultimate kick in the teeth was that he finally admitted that he didn't remember me at all and that I was just some creepy guy he knew he could shake down.

Even now though, I don't feel anger, just sorrow. Still, I know deep down in my heart I did what was inherently the right thing to do. I would rather die today doing the right thing than live a hundred years turning a blind eye. That's something that can't be taken away from me. It's not enough to kill the loneliness though. For that I need a true friend.

There have been some exceptions in my lifetime. There are those that I make true connections with, and though they aren't daily friends, we pick right up where we left off when we do reunite:

There's Sean, who is pretty much the straight version of me without the fabulousness (although,

Singing For No Reason 83

he did get pulled over once for disturbing the peace by playing Kylie Minogue). We met in 1998 and I've never looked up to anyone more. I think we recognized that we both were meant to be the world's reality check. He is more my brother than my two birth brothers, and I like to believe that we live outside the world's normative confines. It's amazing how our lives have traveled down such different paths, and yet he and I remain very much the same. (By the way, if you're wondering where I got my temper from, you have him to thank!)

Lee lives in Denver, well at least Denver-adjacent (#shade). We had speech class together in high school and didn't connect until after we both had graduated. She was always a girl who thought outside of the box and didn't conform to the notion that she needed to be some cheerleader or barefoot and pregnant. It's been about 5 years since I saw her last, but I know we will always have a great drink and good conversation waiting for the both of us.

There never has been and never will be a friend like Jacklyn Joyce. A badass-punk rock-sarcastic-realist-artist-singer-taco-slinger kind of gal. A terrific mother, she gives her heart to everyone one, followed by a Costco sized package of sarcasm. We met in my young adulthood at karaoke and have made each other laugh ever since. If I could describe why we get along so well, I would have to say that we are on the same creative wavelength. She also is the toughest person I've ever met, never letting anyone go over the line. For example, A drunk and pill popping acquaintance once got in her face at 4:00am—and I mean in. her. face.—all the while waving his flip phone. She did what anyone would do: She snatched that phone out of his hand, out of her way and fired it back at him. It broke in half on his face and I loved her through every minute of it. Now I don't condone violence, but he really was on the verge of hitting her. Not to mention he had trashed her room. When things calmed down, we were laying on her bed—a mess now covered in shards of broken mirror. She sighed and commented on how she needed a drink. I quickly replied that I knew of a bar that opened at 7:00am (the time was 6:00am by then). We both laughed so hard that the events of the night just dissolved away, and we fell asleep. If anything, she taught how to laugh in the face of adversity.

I want to make sure that I am not discounting those three angels in this chapter, but they have their own lives (and families) and have scattered to the other corners of the globe. Without them I've had such a hard time making that strong connection with people. Even now with coming out as a Crystal Meth addict, people whom I thought I could count on have banished me from their lives. The chips are down and now my parlor has emptied (guess the new drapes will go unnoticed). I can't describe how much this has hurt me. I often feel like I will never be able to truly make a friend that will see me through thick and thin. And then again, I sometimes think that maybe I did have that chance to find that constant in my life, only to lose it…

…because Davis has gone.

When I moved from my hometown to the closest metropolitan city, I had a severely damaged self-image and had no idea where I was going in life. I had no real plan, because I simply figured I could go back to school whenever I wanted to finish (after all I was an adult now). Big mistake. Seriously: stay in school kids…or else. Starting over once you've stopped isn't as easy as you think it is.

As you'll find out later, my passion is karaoke. One night I found my way to a gay dive bar and, after getting up to sing, earned the attention of a circle of people. They invited me to sit with them, and we had what you would call sort of a "Cheers," camaraderie. That was the closest I had ever felt to belonging in a group.

One person stood out immediately among the others, and his name was Davis. There was never a purer soul so full of life and full of energy. He went out of his way to make me feel welcomed and included. He seemed to want everyone to feel that way. (Upon reflection I suspect he was also an INFP like me).

As it soon turned out, the karaoke host at the bar was quitting, so Davis suggested that I apply to replace him. Against my better judgment, I applied and got the job. I was such a shy introvert, but he said that I was so outgoing and would be perfect for this type of job. I later discovered that although he was aware of the fact that I was probably the least qualified for the job, he still convinced me because he didn't want them to cancel karaoke. I never bought it though, you see. But more important than all that was the fact that I needed to be there anyway, because that was where I would finally begin the journey of finding my voice. My self. He saw what was within and knew this would help bring the real me towards the world outside.

I finally had someone to give my friendship to, not just someone to take from me. Davis was huge into musical theater, and we would spend hours just going over our passion for music. My knowledge of music is pretty much encyclopedic, and I've yet to meet someone that could match wits with me since him. He was trained in ballet and lyrical dance, and as he danced, I would watch his spirit fill the room. He gave 110% percent to all he did, in every aspect of his world. Yet, he was never too busy to share a batch of Lucky Burger onion rings and talk about anything on his or my mind.

The times with Davis were the best times of my life.

Life moved along, as it always does, and suddenly came December of 2006. The musical, "Dreamgirls," was waiting for its turn to premier on the silver screen. The musical was Davis's favorite and one I had never seen. [Insert gay gasp; theater queens clutch your pearls.] I can vividly remember his excitement to be there with me when I would finally experience the big event.

The movie debuted Christmas Day, and I had bought tickets for him and me to go the day after. But I never heard from him. I called and called but received no answer. Finally I ended up going to the movie alone, with an empty seat next to me in a packed theater. And although I really loved the movie (and still I think of it as one of my favorites), I drove home that night, thinking of the mock hell I was going to give Davis. Then, after he would realize I was only kidding, I would go over my favorite parts. I looked forward to it and went to bed that night smiling.

The next day I received a call from an acquaintance informing that Davis had been in the hospital for a week and had passed away.

I stood there alone in silence; the phone just fell from my hand. The next couple of weeks were really a blur. All I remember from the service is that I didn't go up to speak when they invited his friends.

You see, Davis was also HIV positive, but he gave so much to everyone else that his own health responsibilities fell by the wayside. He eventually contracted pneumonia and could not recover.

You may be wondering why I didn't speak at his funeral. It's because I was angry with him. Though I was aware of his status, I had only just come to terms with my own. I did not know how poor his health really was, where he would always just reply, "It's fine Andre," whenever I inquired.

Some would argue that Davis was merely trying to protect me; still I can't help but feel betrayed by his neglecting to come to me with what was going on. I also refamiliarized myself with old feelings of fear and abandonment in light of losing my platform, my rock. My rationalization at the time had been that if Davis was okay, then so was I. He passed away at the age of 32, and I find it peculiar that I am now around the same age and at the same kind of crossroads.

I have since made my peace with Davis's passing, and forgiven both him and myself. I think his final gift to me was to arm me with the forewarning not to repeat his mistakes—to choose the right path at the crossroads we have now both faced. I can't speak to him or know what his final regrets were, but I truly see us as one and the same. That fact alone convinces me that my biggest lesson may also have been his: You cannot be in a successful relationship with others until you can successfully be in one with yourself. This simple lesson is one that so many of us ignore, and without this foundation we tend to build a life like a house of playing cards. So I've started working on relating better to myself. I may never be able to repay all he gave but I'll try.

I sing Davis's songs at karaoke, I honor his spirit and keep his memory alive. You see, my friend now lives on through me. Though I still travel a completely separate path, Davis is a part of that path and because of this I'm hopeful that one day I will encounter my own best self—my own "Andre"—along the way. For when I do, I will give that version of myself all the love and friendship Davis gave me. I miss you old friend, and I love you.

10

The Woman Who Helped Me Become a Man

No, I'm not talking about Meryl. This woman is far more important that any award-winning chameleon. She's one thing and one thing only to me...a crazy bitch. Not in the ex-boyfriend sense, so to the 56,000 guys I've dated please simmer down.

Ladies and gentlemen, it is my greatest pleasure and joy to introduce to you my homegirl: SheBeata Piñata.

Those of you who know me are rolling your eyes so hard with the biggest grin right about now, while the rest of you will just have to bear with me. This is my drag queen alter-ego.

Because I am obsessed with putting words in your mouth, I'm going to tell you what you're thinking: "Big shock Andre, you waited ten chapters to tell us this? We figured out you had one by chapter two."

Give me a break! Surprisingly enough, I had always been one of those guys that swore he would never do drag. I mean famous last words. Deep down there was always a secret curiosity left over from my childhood when I would play dress-up, I assume. Like always I was too scared to even dare to suggest it.

The day after I moved to my current city, I auditioned for a men's chorus. There I experienced an unusual mix of feelings. I had never felt such belonging and such alienation at the same time. But one person took a peculiar interest in me—the person who would be my future drag mother. I'd like to think that she was intrigued.

The name came first.

One night during my first season singing, I was at a party that was winding down. We were all standing in the street, and some chorale members, including my future mother, were talking about the upcoming charity pageant connected with the chorale. Contestants would raise huge amounts of money for AIDS charity, and apparently winning the

Singing For No Reason

title was the kind of feat legends were born from. Someone suggested that I should enter, where I in turn commented that I didn't even have a drag name. My hope was that being nameless would be a quick way to disqualify myself.

Big mistake.

The group instantly began throwing around names, and I found that a lot of the contestants had a thing for double-entendres. But it was out of nowhere that my drag mother blurted out, "SheBeata Piñata" (You get it, don't you? I mean it's obvious). Secretly I loved the name, but I just chuckled and stayed home the day of the pageant.

Two years later I was told I did not have a choice and that there was little interest in the fundraising. The name had stuck with me from that night two years earlier, it lingered like a little devil on my shoulder, and I'm not sure what the hell possessed me, but I caved in and said yes.

Keeping in mind that I had no prior knowledge of the art of drag, you can imagine how "beautiful" I looked that first time. Lord! I cringe! I borrowed wigs, dresses, and got make-up from the dollar store (a very SheBeata thing to do as you'll learn). Then came the talent portion.

To educate the non-drag folk, a drag pageant is much like a beauty pageant in that it has a talent portion where contestants display their gifts. The chorale puts a twist on this though, since 99.8% of the drag world lip-syncs; if you enter this pageant your talent must be anything but a lip sync. A person can sing live, pack a suitcase, or play an instrument. Whatever. The more out of left field it is the more humorous it is.

Since I had a very Latin name, I figured my character should also capture such Latin flavor. Thus I decided my talent would be a cooking demonstration on how to make flour tortillas. This (if I may be frank), turned out to be a total fucking disaster. You see, I figured it would be easier to use the "just add water" tortilla mix. The people in charge of the pageant had made me promise not to make a mess on the dancefloor (the pageant is held at a country western gay bar on the dance floor, I can't make this up people). Amid my act, I held up the bag and poof! The bag burst open and its contents flew everywhere. I don't think I've ever been put on the spot so much in my life. Well I survived and came in dead last.

At first I was discouraged because I felt that, yet again, I was a failure at something. Then something happened that I'd never experienced before. I got mad at myself for not doing a better job. I got hungry for that title and suddenly needed to win more than anything.

I dove in the world of drag. I studied, asked questions and got better. Before long, it was time for the pageant yet again. Although I was much more prepared this time, I was scared of what to do next for the talent part. That's when my drag mother told me to just tell jokes. I instantly gave a puzzled look and commented that I was no comedian. But supposedly I had been hilarious during the whole ordeal that previous year (which I now call "The Great Tortilla Incident"). I agreed, and my talent was listed as "Salvaging Last Year."

Believe it or not, I was funny; I quickly commented that I had no props this time, and that they barely let me have props last year but thought they could trust a Latin girl with a white bag of powder. I looked about 6,000 times better and had fleshed out a real character for this woman. Now I know some might say it's silly to think of SheBeata as a real woman and not a fictional character, but she's definitely real. My other persona is part of me and an extension of who I am—something I didn't realize until much later.

It took two more years for me to win. By then I had a fully-realized version of SheBeata and had learned how happy whenever I was in face (as the kids say). I didn't exactly know why, until one day it hit me. SheBeata was the female version of who I really wanted to be. I thought to myself, "She says whatever she wants, so why can't I?" Through her I was gradually finding myself.

I find it mind-blowing how much drag released my creativity, my humor, my intellect. All because of this undocumented diva. What is most surprising to me is how much strength she has inside of her, a strength that pays tribute to my mother. And it's true, Mom is also where SheBeata got her fashion sense: Believe me if you can make a crepe paper dress look good, you are solidified as a fashion icon.

Even during my addiction, it was SheBeata who kept me company when there was no one there on Thanksgiving Day or Christmas (both of which I spent alone that year). I sat alone riding the train all day to avoid the more chilling elements, coming down from the drug-induced high of days prior by coming up with jokes and skits. The laughter from that kept me warm.

SheBeata belongs to that diverse and amazing drag house formed by my drag mother (who shall remain nameless here to protect her secret crime-fighting identity). It's a real family (and anyone who says otherwise will get their tires slashed by you know who). They were the first full group to support me 110%. Even in hard times. Vividly I remember that the pageant two years after my win would be the one right before my ultimate relapse, where I overdosed. I was a total mess and couldn't get it together, but my drag house came together and helped me bring SheBeata to life one more time. Well I performed, and she looked the best she ever had. More importantly, I laughed and felt normal for the first time in forever. I'd like to think that she was the real reminder to everyone dear to me just how much she and I still had to offer the world and why they stuck by me (us).

It's interesting that SheBeata was born on Cinco De Mayo (May 5th), 2013. That was the night of the first pageant, and the night I like to think that my true self was finally born. My overdose occurred on May 5th, 2017, a day I now consider to mark the death of the old me. I'm a big believer in signs, whether sent by God or not. These form one I just can't ignore.

I have SheBeata to thank for my inner salvation and for the journey together we've just begun. After all, she needs a green card, and finding the right sucker [cough] I mean husband will take some time. So there will definitely be a journey. Still I'm lucky to have her, and it really is as she always says,

> "If you hit the piñata hard enough, the secret of life comes out."

11

Dear Future Husband (Staple This to My Forehead)

I swear. We have become obsessed with it (and I'm not speaking of those idiotic spinners, Pogs were better anyway)! I mean books, movies, CD's, MP3s, Laserdisc, self-help cassettes, smoke signals…They're all about it. Really you people need to get it under control. Seriously. (And by "you" I mean "I."). So let's finally take control of the wheel. Fear not Jesus, I've got this (everyone else: run for your lives!).

While many of you have guessed that I am talking about love, you are only half-right. What I really am getting at is the search to find a successful relationship, in other words, a lasting love. Now, here is my disclaimer: While I have had several memorable relationships, good and bad (the combo ones came with a discount), none have ever lasted long enough be defined as *lasting*.

One could say I've been around the block a few times (No, that is not why the back alley was named after me, not a word!), but I've yet to find the exact recipe for a long and fantastic voyage. Trust me, I have googled till the mouse bled, had my tarot cards read by a naked gay gypsy and have even messaged some monks at the farthest reaches of the Earth only to have come to one irrefutable answer: BEATS THE HELL OUT OF ME.

I do long for a lasting relationship, unique a request as any, but it seems like stuffing at Thanksgiving: Everyone has their own recipe. (God help the ones that throw in the towel and go for the "Stove Top" kind of love, just saying). The only true route towards love that I think has stood the test of time is simple trial and error. Yes, some of us end up getting far more error (and in my case, "Does Not Compute"), so that I can say that even though all of my relationships have had a definitive end, each of them has allowed me to grow. I'm even still friends with a few of my former attachments. Where growth in these relationships is concerned, I speak not only in the positive sense, but in the negative as well. (Yes, my little snarky one, you can grow negatively.)

To put what I am trying to say in layman's terms (or plain English as my ex Alan would say), think of it this way: We grow by learning what qualities or experiences we like in a person, and the same is true of the opposite. We also learn what we do not like and (dare I go so far as to say) what we are *not* willing to compromise on.

There's another one of those terms you hear on commercials for that latest dating app. You know, the ones you watch while drinking your morning coffee. Yes, I know you make fun of those commercials while secretly checking your messages on your own dating site. Compromise is right up there with "Grandma's secret recipe:" Everybody knows somebody who has it down perfectly but nobody knows how to produce it.

I mean seriously though, who has the time to even look at a recipe for great enduring companionship, let alone give it a shot. We are a hurried and selfish society, where instant gratification remains the standard. We expect everything right now and right the first time around (insert "I want to speak to the manager" meme).

I blame Girl Scout cookies. Don't ask me why. I just do.

So, we begin the cocktailian dance of varied partners, some dancing too fast or slow, some going nowhere beyond that tiny circle that is their universe, some with no rhythm whatsoever, and then there are the ones who step on your delicate toes the entire quinceñera (instantly making you regret wearing those open-toed 3-inch heels). The unpredictable steps alone are why most people prefer to watch professional ballroom dancing on TV from the safety of their couches rather than attempting to do so themselves.

Yet again, it's like my grandmother always said,

"Life pays repeatedly when you act out the role for yourself. You get nothing by simply acting it out for others."

Gramo was a wise woman ,and I will fight anyone to the death who says otherwise. I mean she drove a Buick through a brick wall just to prove a point. (Not. One. Word.) My hero. She was the last of a generation that knew the true definition of the word "commitment" in its entirety. Dry spells, lean years, affairs with your sister-in-law's second cousin who was also a beauty queen (at least in her county)… You made the relationship work and never gave up. You don't find them like that anymore, a sad and forgotten truth. (I don't know who I have to butter up, but I am willing to pray to any form of deity—or even make some up if I have to—to find one of the last of this breed).

Yet…if you've read any of the previous chapters, or at least three lines of them, you know I'm not always the best at appreciating what I've been given. Like I said before, life gets in the way. We spend so much time looking down and hyper-involved within our latest iced-coffee-fueled-patriarchal/millennial-society-created problem, that we sometimes forget to look up and across the table. Some of us totally forget that someone is even sitting there. In that kind of setup, how can we ever expect to find anyone beyond whatever screen we're staring at?

Fear not! For a limited time folks, only during this televised special—with this offer code that you have 3 seconds to write down, for that item on QVC you have been hypnotically convinced you need—I am going to tell you how make a successful attempt at a successful relationship (notice my verbiage). This one has been a hit for years and we are so glad they decided to release this special edition just for you viewers at home. (Hi, we're talking to Kathy from Saginaw, Michigan.) So here it is, the key to your pursuit of a successful relationship: Sometimes, we need to remember…YOUR "PROBLEM" CAN WAIT.

You'll have to forgive my stern language, but who are we kidding? You curse worse than three drunken sailors fighting for the last beer and last drunken woman (or drunken man in these progressive days...you go girl). My reason for putting "your problem" in quotes and caps is to help that one simple tool become better engrained in our minds.

Oh! Just so we can get this out of the way, I understand there are five-hundred-twenty-five-thousand-six-hundred other elements that make a good relationship. I've got 37 of them down pat! Some can only be found at that Whole Foods in the mega-rich neighborhood that your single girlfriend shops at religiously to land herself a man. And she *still* always ends up leaving alone with the same singular item (Note to self: Buy stock in boxed wine). Yes, truly successful relating takes such complex effort that an attempt to describe it in steps would not only be ludicrous but also an insult to the actual experience. Alas, beyond the lists of "great advice," we often have to resort to plain old *trust* in order to turn our melody with another into harmony.

"But Andre, you're a part-time sarcastic writer and handsome late-night informercial host. How can a regular person like myself even know where to begin?" Well I'm glad you asked. Here's step one:

Get out there! No one is going to compliment those red sneakers if you don't wear them to your functions (by the way, the man I eventually marry will have red sneakers. Yeah, don't ask. For some unexplained cosmic reason when I think of him wearing red sneakers, I get a smile that lingers the way you'd react to a child who has just learned how to tell a joke). In this day and age of DVR there is no excuse for staying to yourself! Honey just record that *Dancing with the Stars* Latin Night episode (Girl, those men, I know) and get on with it.

Curiously, though I have learned different techniques from past liaisons, the real application will not begin until I meet [insert his name here]. This will be the first man I can say that I have loved. In our epic saga (and I mean "epic" will be an obsolete term by our third date) we will love in what I like to call "reality." Will that be my lifetime-guaranteed spinning mop? Who can say? For you see, time is not important to me when it comes to a true love.

Don't misunderstand me future husband, err I mean readers, I want my true love there every day of this lifetime and the next three (the fourth has been set aside for my personal time. Another important factor). Not to sound too cliché here, but I cannot imagine spending the rest my life alone. Period. Even trying to picture a life in which my partner never arrives becomes so painful that I sometimes get depressed. To the point that it puts a damper on the actual relationship with myself. And there is another lesson in this: If you focus too much on the actual "relationship time" itself, you forget to focus on what you're supposed to *do* with the time! That is, you're so busy imagining the story that you forget to talk to and do things with the person (or yourself) required to write the story in the first place.

So before you start calling me a braggart (I am not perfect, if my credit score is any indication!); know that I often forget not only the vitally important steps, but also the small not-so important ones as well. Trust me, they add up! Luckily, the one thing I have grown to be thankful for (sometimes daily) is that I will never give up. I will always make time to communicate with friends and new associates.

Why make time for others' priorities, you ask? I believe that whatever means something to them, means something to me too. The opposite should also hold true. I consider this to be practice until my guy finally comes to his senses and figures out he cannot live without me.

Yes! I know that there is a possibility we may speak different "love languages," (Okay, am I the only who wants to cast that ridiculous term in the void?). I am optimistic though. Despite our differences, I know we will see and feel the same love for each other.

What really helps is putting effort into whatever the other one cherishes. For me, I cherish watching the same sappy movie for the 9,976th time, I mean *Fried Green Tomatoes* is all I have to say people, am I right? For him, cherishing fried cheese curds may be a thing, renovating an ancient farm house in Wisconsin, and he may have a fanatical obsession with the sport of Volleyball. (God help my hand-eye coordination because I will play volleyball just to make him happy.) And if collecting bicentennial quarters were my partners' hobby, I would save every single one I encountered for him. Eventually I would begin to find them like second nature before long for him just to make him happy. No, I'm not signing up to get walked on, just staying open to trying out things that I might not have known I liked in the beginning. The little things people!

Do I think we will get it right all day every day? No. Though I am hesitant to say so, I know there will be some unpredictable times. Still, I am confident he will put as much effort to work through them as I will. Once we do, I will sincerely and proudly use the term "we" with him.

So how do you uncomplicate those new dance moves of love that the kids are learning from video games nowadays? It's simple. You un-complicate love by simply un-complicating it.

Focus on and learn from the successful times. Don't be defeated by (but also learn from) your not-so-successful ones. Think of it this way: Instead of saying to each other, "Oh my God, we almost didn't make it," you say, "Oh my God, we made it." Honor the hell out of love and put your love for yourself, and your love for your love, above all else. In other words, don't just have a love; have a long-lasting love.

12

The Darkness

I've lived all of my life in the dark. There are no jokes or witty retorts to cover up the seriousness of that statement. I think we live in a time that has diminished what it means to be in the dark. We take an anxiety pill and get on with our day. It's not always that easy for some. The problem is, when you are in the middle of experiencing real darkness yourself, you cannot see, speak or hear.

Most only focus on the light and dark aspects of living in the dark. It's the old good versus evil paradigm. But there is so much more to the dark. Not only are you crawling on the ground looking for a way out, you aren't even aware if there *is* a way out.

Unlike the cases where those deep-sea cameras give us a glimpse of species that dwell on the lightless ocean floors; the reverse is not possible. Those sea creatures have no idea about the world above and, because of that, they do not yearn for it.

Too many times I've heard the phrase, "Why didn't they just reach out?" In my case at least, I didn't know I could. Here is where the "you were told they were there for you," argument comes in, but I was deaf to it. I didn't hear the tornado coming until it was too late. There were no sirens going off when I was trying to shove a needle in my arm with a shaky hand.

I know this is probably a harsh turn from some of the earlier chapters, but it's also an attempt to show just how serious the situation got for me. When friends, acquaintances or even celebrities commit suicide, we are shocked. We wonder how that comedian who made the world laugh his whole life could be so depressed inside. All I've been able to work out is that they were so drained from trying to escape their darkness that death seemed like the only answer. Though this is absurd to some, it will make perfect sense to others. It does to me.

I've committed to being brutally honest, and I must tell you, that I've attempted suicide twice in my life. The first time I was in high school, and I could not take one more day of bullying or ridicule for being gay. The second was during my overdose. I felt totally alone and experienced a psychotic break. Thankfully, I stopped myself both times.

To tell you the truth, I'm afraid of dying. Not of the way I'm going to die, but of what will happen when I do. It's the darkness of my life that has created this fear. For you see, I'm afraid there may be something worse waiting on the other side. A new form of the prison I've already endured for thirty-five years.

I really want you to understand that I'm not just speaking of light and shadow. I'm speaking of the experience of your mind, body and spirit as you feel they are shutting down, retreating into the other direction and into the negative. Darker still, for many of us it's a negative state of being that we didn't know even existed until the descent began.

There are no words in the English language for me to describe the horrors of that kind of life. The darkness is terrifying. You spend your life scared, anxiety-ridden, devastated by one event after another. However, the prison guards aren't done with you yet. No. This is where the darkness becomes a cruel and insidious monster: While you're in it, you can easily find yourself replaying every one of your life's worst moments over and over. From childhood up to now, there they are for your mind to relive and suffer through. The never-ending playback of such things will drive anyone towards desperation.

But I'll stop for now. If I go any further I'll honestly break down crying and will be unable to finish. You may not see it, but I relive it all even while writing this.

So, you may be asking yourself, "Are you still there in the dark?"

There is no real answer for this question, the best I can come up with is "Some days." But you can't imagine the gratitude and thankfulness I feel every morning now that I can finally use all my senses, real and metaphorical. I'd like to say I did it all myself, but it was a team effort.

On the road to fixing myself, it took facing what I had been through and owning every part of it. I also had to find ways to let a lot of it go. There is no need to hold onto the boat full of negative memories that has set sail. If you do, you quickly become the anchor, drowning in the darkness of the sea. Makes sense to me at least.

I kick myself—even right at this moment—at how I consciously added to the list of demons that I had to face. I've faced a lot of them though, one after the other. Gradually I've begun to see that the darkness has a border, seeing traces of light though the bricks—a light that stings at first. As my eyes adjust to the new sight, I am eventually able to perceive my self-image more clearly, blurred but discernable on the other side. I hear a noise beyond the bricks. Sounds that quickly become comprehensible as human voices. I am filled with an exhilarating feeling that there are others in the world. I am, in fact not alone.

Like a wild animal I begin clawing at the wall of darkness, finding gaps in the brick. I start to climb, not knowing if the wall actually ends or if I'm even able to make it over. I make very little headway before I fall hard to the ground. But I keep trying again and again despite falling repeatedly. I refuse to be discouraged, because I now know what's on the other side. I am finally aware that there is an escape from this hell. I reach the ceiling and, with all my might, I punch through the wall, making a small hole. Light suddenly floods my life and I breathe in the fresh air for the first time.

A hand is there to meet me. I look up through the tears in my eyes to see my real self, the true Andre. He is pulling with all his might to get me to where he has been waiting.

I am so heavy though, and the battle begins…But then there are all the people who love me beside him.

There are people who refused to accept what was given, and instead demanded what was true. Even though there have been so many times where I wanted to retreat into my dark world because it's all I've ever known. Miserable as it was, it was at least familiar. But the people who are there for me can recognize the look in my eyes. They've been on their knees, crying, begging for me not to retreat. At the side of my true self they brace themselves and grab my arm, pulling for dear life.

I am especially grateful to the men of the Tortoise Stream Chorale, who have been there all along, consciously or unconsciously, as my salvation. I'm finally able to see them. To hear them. To love them. They have become something tangible to me, and the last seven years have suddenly seemed worth it. The reasons why I stayed around for so long and eventually came back to them are clear as day.

After I told the Chorale about my addiction, and a little while after I had sobered up, I decided I wanted to return to them. I was lying in bed one night and my best friend in the chorale sent a text that he missed me. I couldn't stand it any longer, and I got in the car and drove straight to where they were singing. Once I got there though, I just couldn't go inside. The worst anxiety attack I had ever had hit me right then. I was about to leave when I finally heard their singing. At that moment I closed my eyes and discovered a strength and bravery I'd never known and walked inside. I experienced mixed reactions. Some were supportive but distant, some were flat out rude. Surprisingly, the people who I was afraid would abandon me didn't bat an eyelash after hearing the news. Even more surprising was the fact that some people with whom I had barely spoken pre-meth became wide eyed and ecstatic that I was back. And I sat down, still having the panic attack.

Whether it was my imagination or not, I saw people staring. A couple of them leaned over to their neighbors, whispering. I wanted to leave so badly. But my Big Buddy and friend of seven years, whom I had sat down next to, put his hand on my knee and gave me a smile that said, "Welcome home." From that moment on I was determined.

You know lately I've been noticing something different when I look in the mirror. It's very hard to describe. It's both physical and it's not.

My eyes.

The eyes I had always seen before are somehow gone now. I never reacted when I looked into my eyes in the past. Neither a good nor bad reaction followed. There was nothing. Just eyes. Now there's a deep brown that I find too beautiful to describe. And a genuine depth that envelopes me. In my new reflection I see a well of wisdom and strength that I can now tap into whenever I need to. I merely had to break the dam of self-doubt that was holding it back. I don't mean this in vanity, but when I gaze into those eyes, I feel I can now live the life I was meant to live…

I've only felt this way once before.

Not long after joining the chorale (I think it was my second year), we were having our usual Tuesday night rehearsal. The weather outside was horrific, and having just moved to that area of the country, I was not used to storms so intense. Mid song the lights went out, and I heard sirens going off, the likes of which I had never heard before. Someone next to me informed me that these were tornado sirens, and I immediately became terrified. The folks in charge at the time ordered us all into the hall and stairwell. As we shuffled in, I remained quiet as a tombstone, embarrassed with the fear I was experiencing.

It's amazing how these moments influence the tempo of time. As if in slow motion, the windows were shaking so badly, and I was sure the building was about to collapse, when someone made a joke. A wave of laughter rang out, and then people began talking in smaller groups. Others pulled out their phones and used them as flashlights. Beams of light breaking through the darkness.

Singing For No Reason 117

As I think back to that moment in my career with the chorale, I remember being too distracted by the laughs, good feelings and the gleaming handfuls of light to be scared anymore. I now realize that my fear was neutralized by these. Those boys, those brothers, those Turtles. In that one night, I wasn't afraid of anything, not even death. If a tornado had touched down and ended my life there, I'm sure I would have died happy. In the company of friends, I was living the life I was meant to live, if even for one night.

That is what my friends will always be to me: a light in the darkness. The final element missing in my recovery. A group of people carrying with them a force of light so strong that, together, they've found no struggle in pulling me to them, only to let go and allow me to find strength on my own. You don't always realize how many people you truly have in your corner until you brave the fear and go to where they are. The ones who were never there will disappear, while the ones who were always there will shine brighter than ever, cutting through your darkness. And so I keep going. Finally reaching the surface at the end of my climb, I collapse onto my hands and knees, covered in dirt and filth, gasping for air. Looking up at all of them…

…and smiling.

www.ingramcontent.com/pod-product-compliance
Lightning Source LLC
Chambersburg PA
CBHW071213070526
44584CB00019B/3012